# Judgment Day

ÖDÖN VON HORVÁTH (1901–1938) was born in Fiume, which was then part of the Austro-Hungarian Empire, of an aristocratic Hungarian-speaking family. His plays include: *Italienische Nacht* (*Italian Night*) 1931, *Geschichten aus dem Wiener Wald* (*Tales from the Vienna Woods*) 1931, *Kasimir und Karoline* (*Casimir and Caroline*) 1932, *Figaro Lässt sich Schieden* (*Figaro Gets a Divorce*) 1937, *Don Juan Kommt aus dem Krieg* (*Don Juan Comes Back from the War*), produced 1952. Horváth's plays were banned when the Nazis came to power, then neglected in Germany until the 1950s.

CHRISTOPHER HAMPTON was born in the Azores in 1946. He wrote his first play, *When Did You Last See My Mother?*, at the age of eighteen. Since then, his plays have included *The Philanthropist, Savages, Tales from Hollywood, Les Liaisons Dangereuses, White Chameleon* and *The Talking Cure*. He has translated plays by Ibsen, Molière, von Horváth, Chekhov and Yasmina Reza (including *Art, Life x 3*, and *The God of Carnage*). His television work includes adaptations of *The History Man* and *Hotel du Lac*. His screenplays include *The Honorary Consul, The Good Father, Dangerous Liaisons, Mary Reilly, Total Eclipse, The Quiet American, Atonement, Cheri, Carrington, The Secret Agent* and *Imagining Argentina*, the last three of which he also directed.

ÖDÖN VON HORVÁTH

# Judgment Day

*translated by*
Christopher Hampton

*faber and faber*

First published in 2009
by Faber and Faber Limited
74–77 Great Russell Street, London WC1B 3DA

Typeset by Country Setting, Kingsdown, Kent CT14 8ES
Printed in England by CPI Bookmarque, Croydon, Surrey

A CIP record for this book
is available from the British Library

ISBN 978-0-571-23891-0

2 4 6 8 10 9 7 5 3 1

# Introduction

The critic, Jean-Claude François, memorably described
Ödön von Horváth as 'the black book of the Third Reich':
by which he meant that no other writer documented
more circumstantially than Horváth the day-to-day
experience of life in Nazi Germany in the years leading
up to the Second World War. Bertolt Brecht, for example,
sitting in exile in Scandinavia, wrote of *Fear and Misery
in the Third Reich*, a title which could have covered any
amount of émigré writing; for those in self-imposed exile,
what seemed salient were the crimes and atrocities of the
Nazi régime. But for those, like Horváth, who remained,
what seemed striking was how little the texture of
everyday life had changed, despite the manifest insanity
of the truculently self-righteous posse of morons so
wilfully handed power by the German electorate in 1933.

At the time of the election, Horváth, then thirty-one, was
at the peak of his career and had a powerful new play
*Glaube Liebe Hoffnung (Faith, Hope and Charity)*, in
rehearsal. The play was not allowed to open; Horváth's
parents' house in Bavaria was turned over by the SA
and, like so many other artists, Horváth skipped the
country. He was away for a year: in Budapest, he
renewed his Hungarian passport and in Vienna he
married a Jewish opera singer, Maria Elsner, to provide
*her* with a passport, he later explained. Meanwhile, he
was routinely attacked in the Nazi press: when, in 1931,
he had won the prestigious Kleist Prize, the *Völkischer
Beobachter* described him as a 'Salonkulturbolschewist'
(a high-society Bolshevist) and accused him of staining
the flag of the Reich; and in the same year he was in

court after becoming involved in a brawl with Nazis in a bar. And yet, in 1934, he headed back to Berlin. Why?

He wanted to be able to study National Socialism at close quarters, he said: and so he did. The seven plays and two novels that poured out in the short time remaining to him are a compendium of the petty prejudices and rancourous suspicions of an era of epic mean-mindedness. 'It may seem grotesque,' he wrote, 'at a time like this, unstable as it is, and when no one knows what tomorrow may bring, to set oneself a programme of writing plays. All the same, I make so bold as to do so, even though I have no idea what I'm going to eat tomorrow.'

\*

*Judgment Day* was the last of Horváth's plays to be performed during his lifetime. He missed the premiere, in the unenticing Czechoslovakian town of Mährisch-Ostrau, where the play ran for only four performances, because he was hard at work on his novel, *Ein Kind Unserer Zeit* (*A Child of our Time*). Horváth had turned (or returned) to the novel the previous year, no doubt demoralised by the near-impossibility of getting his plays performed in Germany, and had scored perhaps the greatest success of his career with the novel *Jugend ohne Gott* (Youth without God). This novel is in many ways a companion piece to *Judgment Day*; both are built around a protagonist (in one case a stationmaster; in the other a teacher of history and geography) who lies under oath and then is tormented by his conscience until such time as he confesses; and both have religious and supernatural elements. Both, in other words, deal with guilt: and it may well be that Horváth's project – to describe Nazi Germany from the inside – brought with it a heavy burden of guilt. He had been obliged, for example, in order to be able to take the screenwriting jobs which sustained him in Berlin, to become a member of the Nazi

Writers' Union, the *Reichsverband Deutscher Schriftsteller*, as it called itself with characteristic self-importance.

Guilty or not, Horváth was punished for his success in spectacular fashion. In 1938, when, after the Anschluss, he had finally decided to abandon ship and emigrate to America, he was invited to Paris to discuss, with the director Robert Siodmak, writing a screenplay based on *Youth without God*. After their lunch, encouraged by Siodmak, Horváth took himself off to see *Snow White and the Seven Dwarfs* in a cinema on the Champs Élysées. Afterwards, as he strolled back to his hotel, a sudden storm blew up. Horváth joined a group of people sheltering under a giant chestnut tree outside the Théâtre Marigny; a few moments later he was killed instantly by a falling branch; no one else was injured.

*

For me, *Judgment Day* is the renewal of an old friendship. The first Horváth play I translated, the monumental *Tales from the Vienna Woods*, appeared in the first Olivier Theatre season of the National Theatre, in 1976-7. I worked on a screenplay of this with Maximilian Schell, who directed the film; and then tackled (for the Cottesloe) another of his strange and haunting late plays, never performed in his lifetime, *Don Juan Comes Back from the War*. Then, in the eighties, I made Horváth the central character in my play *Tales from Hollywood*, in which I imagined he had escaped the falling branch on the Champs Élysées and set him down among a group of famous German émigré writers in Los Angeles. Finally, I translated, in 1989, *Faith, Hope and Charity*, which Heribert Sasse directed at the Lyric, Hammersmith.

*Judgment Day* was the first of Horváth's plays to be mounted after the war – in the Theater in der Josefstadt in Vienna. As it happens, that same theatre has revived the play this season and will shortly be premiering my adaptation of *Youth without God*. In the German-speaking theatre (and in France, where a controversial production of his *Kasimir und Karoline* is playing at the Avignon Festival) Horváth has been a constant presence in the repertoire, and his influence on a younger generation of writers – Franz-Xaver Kroetz, Peter Handke, above all Rainer Werner Fassbinder, many of whose films are steeped in Horváth – is incalculable. By contrast, I feel that we in Britain have a long way to go before we could be said to be doing him justice. The old boy is out of copyright now: all the more reason to pay him a little more concentrated attention.

Christopher Hampton
August 2009

**Judgment Day** in this translation was first presented at the Almeida Theatre, London, on 3 September 2009. The cast was as follows:

**Thomas Hudetz** Joseph Millson
**Frau Hudetz** Suzanne Burden
**Alfons** David Annen
**Landlord** Tom Georgeson
**Anna** Laura Donnelly
**Ferdinand** Daniel Hawksford
**Leni** Julie Riley
**Frau Leimgruber** Sarah Woodward
**Woodsman** Andy Williams
**Travelling Salesman** Jack James
**Policeman** Jake Nightingale
**Kohut** Ben Fox
**Public Prosecutor** Patrick Drury
**Deputy** Andy Williams
**Detective** Jack James
**Platelayer** Jack James
**Pokorny** Patrick Drury
**Customer** Ben Fox
**Child** Lewis Lempereur-Palmer, Thomas Patten

*Director* James Macdonald
*Design* Miriam Buether
*Costume Design* Moritz Junge
*Lighting* Neil Austin
*Music* Matthew Herbert
*Sound* Christopher Shutt

# Characters

**Thomas Hudetz**
*stationmaster*

**Frau Hudetz**

**Alfons**
*her brother, a chemist*

**The Landlord**
*of the 'Savage' inn*

**Anna**
*his daughter*

**Ferdinand**
*her fiancé, a butcher from another town*

**Leni**
*waitress at the 'Savage' inn*

**Frau Leimgruber**

**A Woodsman**

**A Travelling Salesman**

**A Policeman**

**Kohut**
*a stoker*

**A Public Prosecutor**

**A Deputy**

**A Detective**

**A Platelayer**

**Pokorny**
*a deceased engine driver*

**A Customer**

**A Child**

# JUDGMENT DAY

*The play is set now (1937).*

*Four months pass between Scenes Two and Three.*

*Interval after Scene Five.*

## SCENE ONE

*We're looking at a railway station: from left to right, a
door leading to the first floor, a booking office, then a door
with frosted glass with the inscription 'Stationmaster'.
Next to this, an array of levers and alarm bells, part of
the signalling system. There are timetables and travel
posters on the wall. Two benches. On the right, the
barrier to one of the platforms runs the depth of the
stage, but the rails are not visible – so that the arrival,
departure and transit of the trains can only be heard.
No express stops here, not even a fast train, because this
is the station for a place not much larger than a village.
It's a small station on a main line.*

*Two passengers are sitting on the benches: the baker's
wife, Frau Leimgruber, and a Woodsman with an empty
rucksack and a tree saw. The signal bell rings; then
everything is quiet again.*

*Now a third passenger arrives left, with a suitcase and
a briefcase: he's a Travelling Salesman from the city. He
stops and looks at the station clock. It's nine o'clock on
a warm spring evening.*

*The Travelling Salesman steps up to the booking office
and knocks, but nothing stirs; he knocks again, putting
some effort into it.*

**Woodsman** Knock till you're blue in the face; he won't
open till just before the train arrives.

**Travelling Salesman** (*looking at the clock again*) Does
that mean the train's late?

**Frau Leimgruber** (*laughing heartily, to the Woodsman*)
How do you answer that question?

3

**Woodsman** (*grinning*) He's come from the moon. (*To the Travelling Salesman.*) Course it's late, three-quarters of an hour late!

**Travelling Salesman** Three-quarters of an hour? Bloody incompetence. (*He lights a cigar, furious.*)

**Frau Leimgruber** It's all a terrible mess . . .

**Woodsman** (*interrupting didactically*) It's because more and more people are being laid off. It's called rationalising, they're going to keep at it till there aren't any trains left at all.

**Travelling Salesman** (*blowing out cigar smoke*) Rationalisation – a sorry state of affairs.

**Woodsman** The best people, they're just chucking them out on the street.

**Frau Leimgruber** (*suddenly becoming garrulous, to the Travelling Salesman*) Give you an example, our station here: how many staff do you think we have, take a guess. One, that's all, one single man.

**Travelling Salesman** (*baffled*) How can that be? Only one man?

**Frau Leimgruber** Fortunately our stationmaster couldn't be more efficient, he's educated, he's polite, a really hard worker, the sort of upstanding young man you don't come across very often! He never shirks, he carries the bags, nails up the crates, works the points, sells the tickets, sends the cables and mans the telephone – all on his own! And the pay is a joke.

**Woodsman** Whose pay?

**Frau Leimgruber** The stationmaster's, of course.

**Woodsman** You call that a joke? I call it a king's ransom – apart from anything else, there's his free accommodation up there! (*He points up at the first floor.*) He's got this big

4

lounge and when he gets up in the morning, he can hear the birds singing and look out at the view . . .

*He grins. The signal bell rings and the stationmaster, Thomas Hudetz, steps briskly out of his door and operates the signal lever; an express train thunders through; he salutes and goes back in.*

**Frau Leimgruber** That was the express, it doesn't stop here.

**Travelling Salesman** I don't blame it. How many people live in this hole?

**Woodsman** Two thousand, three hundred and sixty-four.

*Silence.*

**Frau Leimgruber** (*eyeing the Travelling Salesman, abruptly*) Didn't you like our town?

**Travelling Salesman** My dear lady, I'm a travelling salesman and fate has carried me to every corner of the globe, but I must say, I don't think I've ever experienced such a dazzling display of apathy as I've found here! Quite exceptional!

**Frau Leimgruber** What are you selling?

**Travelling Salesman** Cosmetic supplies.

**Woodsman** Eh?

**Travelling Salesman** Beauty products.

**Woodsman** Beauty, eh? (*He grins.*) Perhaps we're beautiful enough.

**Travelling Salesman** Well, if you're happy, that's the main thing . . .

*He turns to Frau Leimgruber.*

One single customer took pity on me . . . (*A pained smile.*)

5

**Frau Leimgruber** (*very curious*) Who was that?

**Travelling Salesman** The young waitress at the 'Savage' inn.

**Woodsman** (*surprised*) Leni? Not possible!

**Travelling Salesman** (*baffled*) Why not?

**Woodsman** She's not stupid, you wouldn't catch her letting herself be talked into all that beauty bollocks.

**Travelling Salesman** (*flaring up*) Do you mind! This is the twentieth century . . .

**Frau Leimgruber** (*interrupting him, to the* Woodsman) This gentleman ought to know who his customers are.

**Travelling Salesman** (*indignantly*) Little slim thing she was – not much more than a child.

**Frau Leimgruber** (*to the* Woodsman) Oh, he means Anna!

**Woodsman** That makes sense!

**Frau Leimgruber** (*to the Travelling Salesman, garrulously*) She's not a waitress, Anna, she's the landlord's daughter! She's engaged to a butcher, but he's from out of town, he only comes by once a week.

**Travelling Salesman** You don't say.

**Woodsman** She knows what's what, that's all I can say.

**Frau Leimgruber** (*startled*) Who?

**Woodsman** Anna, of course. (*Sarcastically.*) Not much more than a child!

**Frau Leimgruber** How can you say such a thing? Anna, she's innocence personified in person.

**Woodsman** She may be innocent, but she still knows what's what.

**Frau Leimgruber** (*to the Travelling Salesman*) That's how innocent people get a bad reputation.

**Travelling Salesman** (*half to himself*) The rise of the proletariat. The decline of the West . . .

*The stationmaster's wife, Frau Hudetz, emerges from the door on the left with her brother Alfons, the chemist.*

**Frau Leimgruber** (*greeting her*) Good evening, Frau Hudetz!

**Frau Hudetz** Good evening, Frau Leimgruber.

*She has a quiet conversation with Alfons. Frau Leimgruber attempts to eavesdrop, but can't make anything out; she turns to the Travelling Salesman, who has sat down next to her, and points discreetly to Frau Hudetz.*

**Frau Leimgruber** (*in an undertone*) That's the station-master's wife.

**Travelling Salesman** (*uninterested*) Interesting.

**Frau Leimgruber** And the man's her brother.

**Travelling Salesman** (*not bothering to look*) Ah.

**Frau Leimgruber** (*vindictively*) Brother and sister, made for each other . . .

*The signal bell rings again and Hudetz steps briskly out of his door, operates the signal lever again and a train thunders through; he salutes and turns to leave, is surprised to see his wife and Alfons; the two men look at each other for a moment, then Alfons greets Hudetz, who acknowledges him and goes back in his door.*

**Frau Hudetz** (*quietly, to Alfons*) He hasn't spoken to me for days.

**Alfons** Chin up, dear.

**Frau Hudetz** You watch, he'll drive me mad.

**Alfons** You're just under a strain because you're fighting all the time.

**Frau Hudetz** But I keep hearing these voices . . .

**Alfons** (*cutting her off*) There has never been a single case of mental illness in our family. You're in a purely nervous state of emotional over-excitement, that's all, any doctor could tell you that. I'm afraid your marriage is what's called a Gordian knot, there's only one solution.

**Frau Hudetz** (*interrupting him*) Stop it! I'm not even going to think about it, so he can go off with another woman – I said to him before we got married: think carefully, I said, I'm thirteen years older than you and he said, nothing to think about.

**Alfons** (*cutting her off*) He was lying.

**Frau Hudetz** Not then he wasn't.

*Silence.*

**Alfons** It's never been right between you two.

**Frau Hudetz** But I'm not going to get a divorce, do you understand, I'd rather my hair turned white overnight, all white . . .

**Alfons** Not so loud.

*He glances suspiciously at Frau Leimgruber and then resumes talking quietly with Frau Hudetz. Frau Leimgruber speaks quietly to the Travelling Salesman, who is now deep in his account books, making calculations and hardly listening.*

**Frau Leimgruber** She's such a swine – very unpopular woman – never stops tormenting that poor stationmaster, he's a saint, he's so kind – it's an absolute disgrace.

**Travelling Salesman** Really.

**Frau Leimgruber** Never stops tormenting the poor man, she's sick with jealousy, he hardly dares show his face at the 'Savage' any more, she comes creeping after him and if she catches him looking at the waitress, there's hell to pay when she gets him home . . .

**Travelling Salesman** Really.

**Frau Leimgruber** She made such a fuss there on Valentine's Day, yelling her head off, you could hear it down in the village, hysterical bitch – he never laid a finger on her and she kept bellowing: 'He's murdering me, he's murdering me!' My God, she needs her bottom spanking till her teeth rattle.

**Travelling Salesman** (*suddenly paying attention*) Whose bottom?

**Frau Leimgruber** (*offended*) Here I am, giving you all these intimate details, and you're not even listening.

**Travelling Salesman** Well, excuse me.

   *Silence.*

**Alfons** (*quietly, to Frau Hudetz*) Why don't you go away for a few days – look at that poster, it doesn't cost much to go to the seaside these days.

**Frau Hudetz** (*bitterly*) More than I can afford.

**Alfons** I could lend you some money, I have a bit put by.

**Frau Hudetz** (*smiling*) No, you're the best there is, if only people knew how kind you are.

**Alfons** I'm no saint. As for what people think . . .

**Frau Hudetz** People are unbearable.

**Alfons** I know what you mean.

**Frau Hudetz**  Far as I'm concerned, they can all rot in hell . . .

**Alfons** (*smiling*) That's putting it a bit strong.

**Frau Hudetz** (*smiling sweetly*) I mean it, the lot of them. Goodbye, dear.

**Alfons**  Think about it, few days at the seaside if you like.

**Frau Hudetz** (*all of a sudden, tough and serious*) No, I'm staying. Bye, Alfons.

*She goes back in the door on the left. The Travelling Salesman notices Alfons for the first time and stares at him. Alfons is watching Frau Hudetz go.*

**Alfons** (*murmuring, almost to himself*) Goodbye.

*He goes out left, lost in thought. The Travelling Salesman watches him leave and turns back to Frau Leimgruber.*

**Travelling Salesman**  Wasn't that the chemist?

**Frau Leimgruber**  Himself.

**Travelling Salesman**  Pretty unpleasant piece of work, judging by the way he treated me today.

**Frau Leimgruber**  How was that?

**Travelling Salesman** (*shrugging his shoulders*) Not so easy to explain.

*Silence.*

**Frau Leimgruber**  Yes, he's very unpopular as well, the chemist.

**Travelling Salesman**  Not surprised.

**Frau Leimgruber**  He and his sister, people keep out of their way. They always have such stuck-up, insulted looks on their faces, you start feeling guilty, as if you'd done something to them – but it's not my fault he lost his fortune in the inflation or that she forced the stationmaster into an unhappy marriage – she's thirteen years older than he is.

**Travelling Salesman** (*cutting her off*) Thirteen years?

**Frau Leimgruber** She seduced that upstanding, educated young man, when he was still no more than a boy. Woman's a disgrace.

**Travelling Salesman** Ah, well, women, yes, they bring you into the world and then they do their best to bundle you out of it.

*Now Ferdinand, the butcher from out of town, arrives, with his fiancée, Anna, the landlord's daughter. They enter hurriedly from the left, both somewhat out of breath, as they've been running. Ferdinand hurries up to the Woodsman, who for some time has been apathetically munching a large hunk of bread, without a thought in his head.*

**Ferdinand** Have we missed the train?

**Woodsman** Ha!

**Anna** (*to Ferdinand*) See, what did I tell you, it's always late.

**Ferdinand** You shouldn't rely on it being late.

**Anna** (*putting her hand on her heart*) God, you can tell I've been running.

**Ferdinand** (*concerned*) Is your little heart hurting?

**Anna** No, it's just beating so fast . . .

*Ferdinand puts his hand on her heart and listens.*

**Anna** Can you hear it?

**Ferdinand** Yes.

**Frau Leimgruber** (*quietly, to the Travelling Salesman*) There's Anna.

**Travelling Salesman** Anna who?

**Frau Leimgruber** Not much more than a child, you said.

**Travelling Salesman** (*recognising Anna*) Oh, yes, the landlord's daughter. My only customer . . .

*He greets Anna, murmuring as he does so.*

She walks in beauty like the sun . . .

*Anna acknowledges him shyly.*

**Ferdinand** (*to Anna, suspiciously*) Who's that?

**Anna** I'm not telling.

**Ferdinand** Why not?

**Anna** Because you'll start shouting at me again.

**Ferdinand** I never shout at you.

**Anna** Huh!

*Ferdinand glances at the Travelling Salesman.*

**Travelling Salesman** (*becoming uncomfortable; quietly to Frau Leimgruber*) Who is that and why's he staring at me that way?

**Frau Leimgruber** That's Anna's out-of-town fiancé. His name's Ferdinand Bichler, he's a butcher.

**Travelling Salesman** (*feeling even more uncomfortable*) A butcher, is it?

**Frau Leimgruber** A great hulking brute, but really gentle.

*Hudetz opens the booking office.*

**Travelling Salesman** (*sigh of relief*) At last!

*He moves over to the booking office and buys a ticket.*

**Ferdinand** (*to Anna*) If you don't tell me right this minute, I'm going to break his neck.

**Anna** (*smiling*) All right, all right: he's the travelling salesman I bought that cream from this morning.

**Ferdinand** (*reassured*) I see. But you don't need any cream or any powder or anything . . .

**Anna** (*interrupting him*) Don't start that again.

*Silence.*

**Ferdinand** (*rather meekly*) Annie. All I mean is your cheeks are so soft and rosy, no make-up in the world could ever . . .

**Anna** You remember that film we saw last time. God, that woman was so beautiful.

**Ferdinand** I didn't think so.

**Anna** Don't say that. You're just showing yourself up.

*Silence.*

**Ferdinand** (*sadly*) Oh, Anna.

*He puts his arm round her shoulder and looks upwards.*

You know, when I see our little star up there, I wish I could be with you all the time.

**Anna** (*also looking upwards*) You'll see me soon enough.

**Ferdinand** (*nodding sadly*) In a week. And tomorrow back to the grind, up with the lark at four o'clock.

**Anna** Are you slaughtering tomorrow?

**Ferdinand** Couple of veal-calves, that's all . . .

*The signal bell rings, Hudetz steps briskly out of his
door and opens the barrier to the platform; the
Woodsman, Frau Leimgruber and the Travelling
Salesman all process on to the platform, as Hudetz
punches their tickets.*

**Travelling Salesman** (*to Hudetz*) Is that the way it works
here? Three-quarters of an hour late?

*Hudetz shrugs his shoulders and smiles.*

Incompetence . . .

**Frau Leimgruber** (*to the Travelling Salesman*) Don't
blame the stationmaster, it's not his fault.

*Hudetz smiles at Frau Leimgruber and politely touches
his cap. The slow train arrives and pulls up.*

**Ferdinand** (*to Anna*) Mind you don't forget me!

*He embraces her and hurries on to the platform.
Anna moves slowly up to the barrier.
Hudetz gives the signal for departure.
The train pulls out, the signal bell rings.
Anna waves slowly as the train pulls out.
Hudetz closes the barrier.*

**Anna** (*looking at him suddenly*) Didn't anyone get off?

**Hudetz** No.

*He operates the signal and sets off back towards his
door.*

**Anna** Herr Hudetz. Why don't you come and visit us any
more? My father thinks you must have started going
somewhere else.

**Hudetz** I don't go anywhere any more, Fräulein Anna.
I'm always on duty.

**Anna** Well, that's all right, then. I thought perhaps you'd stopped coming because of me.

**Hudetz** (*genuinely surprised*) Why because of you?

**Anna** I thought, because of your wife.

**Hudetz** What's my wife to do with you?

**Anna** She doesn't like me.

**Hudetz** Go on, you're imagining things.

*He stops abruptly and looks up at the first floor. Silence.*

**Anna** (*ironically*) What's up there?

**Hudetz** Nothing.

**Anna** Afraid your wife might see you with a young girl? Aren't you allowed to talk to me?

**Hudetz** You think you know everything.

**Anna** If you talk to me now, there'll be hell to pay tomorrow, isn't that true?

**Hudetz** Who says?

**Anna** Everybody.

*Silence.*

**Hudetz** (*staring at her*) You really all ought to leave my wife in peace, understand? All of you, especially you, Fräulein Anna. You're much too young to get involved in all this . . .

**Anna** (*mockingly*) Is that so?

**Hudetz** There's a lot of things you'll never learn, until you start to understand . . .

**Anna** (*as before*) Oh, yes, give us a little lesson, will you, teacher . . .

**Hudetz**  The first thing you have to learn is if you don't want to hurt yourself, don't hurt other people.

**Anna**  Now you're sounding like the priest . . .

*She laughs.*

**Hudetz**  Have a good laugh, we'll speak another time . . .

*He starts to leave.*

**Anna**  Everybody's laughing at you, Herr Hudetz. What's he really up to, they say, attractive man like that – stuck in his station morning, noon and night . . .

**Hudetz**  (*fiercely*) People seem unusually interested in me.

**Anna**  Yes, what they're saying is, the stationmaster isn't a man at all.

*Silence.*

**Hudetz**  Who says that?

**Anna**  Everybody. I'm the only one who defends you, sometimes.

*She smiles maliciously, kisses him suddenly and points up at the first floor.*

Now she's seen me kissing you, how about that? (*She laughs.*) Now what's going to happen? (*She laughs.*) Now you'll be for it, won't you?

*She makes a spanking gesture.*

**Hudetz**  (*staring at her*) If you don't clear off this minute, you're going to be in big trouble!

**Anna**  You want to kill me?

**Hudetz**  Stop this stupid nonsense and get out!

*He grabs her arm.*

**Anna** Ow, let go of me, you thug!

*She pulls herself free and rubs her arm.*

Can't you take a joke?

**Hudetz** (*roughly*) No!

*An express train passes through.*

Christ Almighty!

*He throws one of the signal levers, the signal bell rings, he clutches at his heart.*

**Anna** (*frightened*) What is it?

**Hudetz** (*staring in front of him, a whisper*) That was express train 405 and I forgot the signal . . . (*He snaps at her.*) There's your joke for you. I've always followed orders and done my duty!

**Anna** It's all right, nothing's going to happen.

**Hudetz** Shut up!

*He goes back in the door.*


### SCENE TWO

*Express train 405, which had not been given a signal, collided, not far from the little station, with a goods train. We are at the site of the accident. There's twisted wreckage on the embankment in the background. The injured and dead have already been removed. Sappers are working on clearing the track. Downstage right is a little black table with a lamp. The Public Prosecutor and his staff have been working for some time; at the moment he's inspecting the signal on the embankment, which is set at red.*

17

*Sightseers have arrived from all over the region; they include the Landlord of the 'Savage' inn, his daughter Anna and his waitress Leni. Downstage left, a Policeman with fixed bayonet is keeping the inquisitive at bay.*

*Dawn is breaking, it's going to be a grey day. There's a chill in the air.*

**Policeman** Back. Get back, will you! You can't get enough of it, can you, when there's a disaster.

**Landlord** It's not every day you see something like this . . .

**Leni** (*to the Policeman*) Did it jump the rails?

**Policeman** No, it was a collision. The express hit a goods train – five and a half hours ago.

**Leni** Horrible! Like the end of the world . . .

*She clings on to the Landlord for some unknown reason.*

I'm going to have nightmares . . .

*The Landlord automatically presses Leni close to him.*

**Landlord** It's the hand of God, all the way.

*Now the Stoker of the crashed train appears; he's wearing a bandage round his head.*

**Leni** (*to the Landlord*) Look, he's injured!

**Stoker** (*nodding genially to Leni*) That's right, and a few inches one way or the other and it would have been thank you and goodnight. I didn't have a thought in my head, all of a sudden there was this hellish crash and jolt, and I was flying through the air like an aeroplane and then everything went black – and when I woke up, I was lying in a meadow in the hay, every bone intact. Just my head buzzing and spinning like a wheel.

**Landlord** You must have a very special guardian angel.

**Stoker** Anything's possible; see, I'm standing in the locomotive . . .

**Leni** (*interrupting him*) Are you the driver?

**Stoker** No, I'm not Pokorny, poor soul. My name's Kohut.

**Policeman** (*to Leni*) He's only the stoker!

**Landlord** Ah.

**Stoker** A stoker's very important as well, let me tell you. Quite often, the stoker's more important than the driver.

**Leni** (*to the Stoker*) Is it true there were over a hundred people killed?

**Stoker** Seventeen, I heard.

**Policeman** (*to the Stoker*) I was told eighteen.

**Landlord** That's enough to be getting on with.

**Stoker** Apparently he went through a signal, or rather the signal was never given, or rather it was only given once he'd gone past – in other words, too late! The Public Prosecutor's been there for three hours, he's having a good look at it, the signal. For the hundredth time.

**Landlord** And whose fault is it?

**Policeman** That will eventually crystallise.

**Stoker** I'd say the stationmaster.

**Landlord** Hudetz?

**Stoker** Don't know what he calls himself. All I know is Pokorny, God rest him, was a completely reliable engine driver, always did his duty – eyes like a lynx, he had.

**Landlord** Well, it would be very strange if our Hudetz had done something wrong! Out of the question, I'd say.

**Stoker**  It'll all come out in the wash. If your Hudetz didn't set the signal in time – he won't be out for a good three years.

**Policeman**  And he'll be out of a job.

**Stoker**  And lose his pension.

**Policeman**  As you'd expect.

**Stoker**  He needs a witness, he has to have a witness who'll swear he set the signal in time.

**Policeman**  Then he'd be saved. But he was on his own, not a soul around.

**Stoker**  Then it's what you call a personal tragedy.

**Anna** (*quietly, to the Landlord*) Father, I need to speak to you . . .

**Landlord**  What's up?

**Anna**  It's important. The stationmaster wasn't alone when it happened . . .

**Landlord**  What? What are you raving on about?

**Anna**  The stationmaster might have a witness . . .

**Landlord**  What? Come on, spit it out!

**Anna**  Me. I was at the station when it happened.

**Landlord**  You? At the station?

**Anna**  Not so loud! I took Ferdinand to the station and then I had a chat with the stationmaster, only a few words . . .

**Landlord**  Yes? And?

**Anna** (*very quietly*) And . . .

   *She whispers to him, inaudible.*

**Leni**  Are there still bodies in the wreckage?

**Stoker** What do you think, miss?

**Leni** No more injured?

**Stoker** Come on! If there was injured there, they'd be screaming their heads off, you'd have to put your hands over your ears!

**Policeman** You said it!

*He laughs. The Public Prosecutor arrives with his Deputy, bleary-eyed and shivering; he's followed at a distance by Hudetz, escorted by another Policeman with fixed bayonet.*

Here's the Public Prosecutor! Back, everyone, stand back!

*He pushes the Landlord, Anna, Leni and the rest of the sightseers over to the left; only the Stoker remains. The Public Prosecutor speaks quietly to the Deputy, so that Hudetz can't hear him.*

**Public Prosecutor** I'm afraid there's nothing wrong with the signal, it's set on half. There's no way of proving whether it was set before or after the train went through.

**Deputy** The only people who could have told us are unfortunately no longer available.

**Public Prosecutor** It's so stupid! I have a funny feeling this Hudetz isn't entirely innocent. He's very calm . . .

*He smiles.*

**Deputy** (*grinning*) A little too calm, if you ask me.

**Public Prosecutor** (*sighing*) Now, let's try again for the tenth time . . .

*He sits at the little black table and thumbs through the reports. A Detective hurries in from the right and grabs the Public Prosecutor.*

**Detective** I've come straight from the station, sir, I've been interviewing Frau Hudetz. I've got a funny feeling she has something to tell us . . .

**Public Prosecutor** 'A funny feeling', is that the best you can do? I need something a little more scientific.

**Detective** Sorry, sir, but I've learned to trust my intuition sometimes and if Frau Hudetz isn't holding something back, I'll eat my hat.

**Public Prosecutor** Where d'you get this idea?

**Detective** Something seems to be troubling her – looks as if she might have been crying.

**Public Prosecutor** Bring her here!

**Detective** Right away, sir!

*He hurries out, right.*

**Public Prosecutor** (*calls out*) Herr Kohut! Josef Kohut!

**Stoker** (*stepping forward*) Present!

**Public Prosecutor** (*very quietly, so that Hudetz can't hear him*) You're sticking with what you said, you didn't see the signal? Keep your voice down.

**Stoker** I didn't see anything, sir, I was standing facing backwards shovelling coal and there was this jolt . . .

**Public Prosecutor** (*interrupting him impatiently*) Yes, you've already told us about the jolt.

**Stoker** Apart from the jolt, I don't have anything to tell you, I can only assure you again that Pokorny, God rest him, has never driven through a signal, not even in the thickest fog!

**Public Prosecutor** That's right, he has a first-class record.

**Stoker** He was a first-class man, sir, that good-hearted, now he's left three children behind with no one to provide for them . . . (*He looks upwards.*) Pokorny, you poor soul! There you stand, in front of the judgment seat.

**Public Prosecutor** Can we stick to the point?

**Stoker** Well then, when the jolt happened, Pokorny was in the middle of talking about his pay rise . . .

**Public Prosecutor** (*interrupting him*) That's not relevant to us. Thank you, Herr Kohut.

**Stoker** (*bowing*) Not at all, not at all.

*He leaves.*

**Public Prosecutor** (*calls out*) Herr Thomas Hudetz!

*Hudetz steps forward.*

You're sticking with what you said, that you set the signal on half at the correct time?

**Hudetz** (*calm, but masking an inner insecurity*) I can't imagine I didn't, sir, I've always followed orders and done my duty . . .

**Public Prosecutor** (*interrupting him*) You've already told us that, I don't know how many times.

**Hudetz** That's all I have to say.

*Silence.*

**Public Prosecutor** (*staring at him; quietly, but insistently*) I can't shake this funny feeling . . .

**Hudetz** (*interrupting him*) I have nothing to hide.

*Silence.*

**Public Prosecutor** (*wagging a finger at him*) Herr Hudetz, a fatal collision is a serious matter . . .

**Hudetz** (*shaken, but attentive*) Sir . . .

**Public Prosecutor** (*suddenly shouting at him*) Don't imagine the truth won't come to light. Even though the driver and the guard were both killed, which was an extraordinary piece of luck for you, there is still one person who miraculously survived. The stoker, Josef Kohut! And the stoker has been able to share some extremely pertinent facts with us, facts you would not be very happy to hear, I can promise you that.

**Hudetz** (*uncertainly*) I can only tell you, I've never missed a signal in my life . . .

*He smiles. Silence.*

**Public Prosecutor** (*suddenly paternal*) Look into your heart, Thomas Hudetz. Think of those eighteen poor victims, think of a whole host of seriously injured, lying suffering in hospital. Do you want to lug all that around for the rest of your life, unatoned for? You're a decent man, Herr Hudetz. Why don't you ease your conscience . . . ?

*Silence.*

**Hudetz** It wasn't my fault.

**Public Prosecutor** (*sarcastically*) Then whose was it?

**Hudetz** Not mine.

**Public Prosecutor** (*as before*) Maybe it was a person or persons unknown?

**Hudetz** Maybe . . .

*The Policeman, the Landlord and Anna arrive from the left.*

**Deputy** (*to the Policeman*) Yes, what is it?

*The Public Prosecutor listens in.*

**Policeman** Sir, the landlord of the 'Savage' came and told me his daughter has an important announcement to make.

24

**Public Prosecutor** (*cutting him off*) And? Why's she waited till now?

**Landlord** Sir, my daughter is not much more than a child and she didn't have the confidence at first, so to start off with she confided in me and I said you have to come forward right away, because this might be a matter of life or death for our friend Herr Hudetz . . .

**Public Prosecutor** Wait and see, shall we?

**Landlord** I said to her, this has to do with a man's future, you'd never have a minute's peace and neither would I, if anything happened to our friend Herr Hudetz. She saw it, sir, with her own eyes, she saw him set the signal on half in good time!

**Public Prosecutor** In good time? (*He stares at Anna.*) Step closer, Fräulein. Don't be afraid, we won't bite . . .

*Anna comes closer.*

Let me make it clear that everything you say here will have to be repeated in court under oath. You understand what that means?

**Anna** Yes.

*Hudetz is staring at Anna, flabbergasted.*

**Public Prosecutor** (*leaning back*) Now, tell us what you know.

**Anna** He set the signal in plenty of time . . .

**Public Prosecutor** (*interrupting her*) One thing at a time and start at the beginning. Off you go.

*Silence.*

**Anna** (*as if reciting a school exercise*) Yesterday I took my fiancé to catch the last train which was very late and I waved to him till the train was out of sight and then

I had a few words with the stationmaster, I asked him why he'd stopped coming to visit us, he doesn't go anywhere any more . . .

**Public Prosecutor** What's that got to do with you?

**Anna** My father's the landlord, obviously I'm concerned about the business.

*She smiles.*

**Landlord** (*to the Public Prosecutor*) Excuse me interrupting, but the stationmaster never goes anywhere any more, because his wife won't let him.

**Public Prosecutor** (*pricking up his ears*) His wife?

**Landlord** You know what I mean, sir, by a shrew?

**Public Prosecutor** (*sighing*) I do.

**Hudetz** My wife is not a shrew.

**Landlord** Leave off, Hudetz! (*To the Public Prosecutor.*) He's always defending her, drives you demented. (*To Hudetz.*) She's on your back from morning to night!

**Hudetz** She isn't!

**Landlord** Leave off! Everybody knows!

**Hudetz** You don't know anything, anything at all! There are reasons for everything and you're not in a position to judge. A lot of it's my fault, I haven't been able to . . .

**Landlord** He hardly dares cross the street, sir, he thinks everything's his fault, because it's been drummed into him from morning to night, year in year out. And what's the reason? It's just that their relationship's gone off the boil, if you know what I mean, hardly surprising, given the age difference.

**Hudetz** (*shouting at the Landlord*) That's got nothing to do with it!

**Landlord** (*to Hudetz*) Don't you shout at me!

**Public Prosecutor** Order! Herr Hudetz, it says a great deal for your integrity that you're so valiantly standing up for your wife and the investigating authorities are pleased to take note of this, all the same it wouldn't necessarily help matters to give way to self-delusion . . .

**Hudetz** (*cutting him off*) I'm not deluding myself.

**Public Prosecutor** Let's leave your wife out of it now, shall we? You'll be seeing the psychiatrist anyway . . .

**Landlord** She's driven him round the bend, right round the bend!

**Public Prosecutor** Order! (*To Anna.*) Carry on, Fräulein.

**Anna** I've nearly finished. I heard the signal bell ring, then the stationmaster set the signal, and after that the express train came through . . .

**Public Prosecutor** After that?

**Anna** Yes . . .

*Frau Hudetz appears, right, with the Detective. They stop and listen, unnoticed by the others.*

**Public Prosecutor** (*insistently*) So: first the signal bell?

**Anna** And then the signal.

**Public Prosecutor** And only then the train?

**Anna** Yes. And then . . .

*She breaks off.*

**Public Prosecutor** Yes?

**Anna** And then in the distance it was like thunder, a crashing and thundering and a kind of wailing – a terrible kind of wailing, oh, I can still hear it now . . .

*She covers her ears.*

**Public Prosecutor** Herr Hudetz. Why didn't you tell us you had a witness for the defence?

*Hudetz doesn't know what to say.*
*Frau Hudetz is watching Hudetz, her expression malicious.*

**Public Prosecutor** Well?

*Hudetz shrugs his shoulders.*

Strange.

**Anna** Well sir, he didn't know I'd seen everything . . .

**Frau Hudetz** (*harshly*) Seen everything?

*This startles everybody; they all look at Frau Hudetz.*

**Detective** (*to the Public Prosecutor*) Frau Hudetz.

**Public Prosecutor** Ah.

*Frau Hudetz is staring vindictively at Anna.*

**Detective** (*quietly, to the Public Prosecutor*) There's nothing to be got out of her. She says she didn't see anything. She was already asleep . . .

*He continues to speak, inaudible.*

**Frau Hudetz** (*to Anna*) You were just trying to provoke me, weren't you?

**Landlord** (*to Frau Hudetz*) What do you want with my daughter?

**Frau Hudetz** (*to Hudetz, pointing at Anna*) Is that your witness for the defence? Well done, well done.

*She grins.*

**Landlord** Frau Hudetz, shut your mouth.

**Frau Hudetz** I wasn't speaking to you.

**Landlord** And don't be so superior.

**Frau Hudetz** I don't have to take instructions from you. You'd be better off teaching your daughter not to spend her nights knocking about with strange men.

**Landlord** What did you say? Knocking about, my daughter? Frau Hudetz, I advise you not to play games with me!

**Public Prosecutor** Frau Josefine Hudetz, step closer.

*Frau Hudetz comes closer.*

You've nothing you want to tell us?

*Frau Hudetz looks witheringly at Hudetz and Anna.*

**Frau Hudetz** (*after a pause*) No!

**Public Prosecutor** Heard nothing, saw nothing, thank you very much. We don't need you any more. Off you go . . .

*He leafs through his reports. Frau Hudetz starts to go.*

**Landlord** (*to Frau Hudetz*) Come on, *avanti, avanti*!

*Frau Hudetz stops in her tracks and stares at the Landlord, seething with rage.*

(*Ironically.*) We don't need you any more. On your bike!

**Frau Hudetz** (*suddenly explodes*) I'm not going! I'm not going! I refuse to let you treat me like this. You think you can do what you like with me, with me and my poor brother. No, I'm not going to take it lying down any more, I'll say what I like, I'll say what I like.

**Landlord** Shut up!

**Frau Hudetz** You're not going to tell me to shut up. Better tell your precious daughter to shut up, before she commits perjury. That's right, I'm going to testify now, it's my turn! Yesterday evening, sir, I was standing at my first-floor window and I saw everything and I heard everything. Everything, everything, everything! I saw quite clearly this slut kissing my husband – I saw it!

**Landlord** Kissing . . . ? Right, that's it!

**Anna** (*suddenly letting fly*) She's lying, she's lying, she's lying!

**Frau Hudetz** I'm telling the truth and I'll swear to it in court. She kissed him just to provoke me, but there's a God of vengeance and that's why he forgot the signal – I'll swear to it, I'll swear to it, I'll swear to it . . .

**Anna** (*beside herself, yelling at her*) Swear, go on, swear, perjure yourself! You're a wicked woman. Just because you're too old for your husband, you've decided to drop him in it, you're trying to do away with him altogether, just because he won't touch you any more. You're notorious, you are, and I never gave him a kiss, so help me, God. I'm very happily engaged, but she just wants to make everybody unhappy . . .

*She bursts into sudden violent sobs and buries her head in her father's chest. The Landlord strokes her hair.*

**Public Prosecutor** I hope it's quite clear to you, Frau Hudetz, your statement is extremely damaging to your husband.

**Landlord** (*furiously to Frau Hudetz*) You should be ashamed of yourself, especially when he's always defending you.

**Anna** (*sobbing, to Frau Hudetz*) He's always defending you! Always!

**Frau Hudetz** Defending me? (*She grins sarcastically.*) Are you always defending me, Thomas?

**Hudetz** Yes.

**Landlord** (*to Hudetz*) And does she deserve it?

**Hudetz** No.

**Landlord** Well, then.

**Hudetz** Sir, everything my wife has accused me of is lies. Fräulein Anna never kissed me and I did not forget the signal. My wife is not quite herself.

**Frau Hudetz** Not myself? That'd suit you, wouldn't it?

**Hudetz** (*to the Public Prosecutor*) When she's alone, she often hears voices – she's told me about it herself. And her brother.

**Frau Hudetz** You're not going to get rid of me like that. Not me.

**Hudetz** I will now – if a wife tries to incriminate her own husband . . .

**Frau Hudetz** (*interrupting him*) 'Husband', what's this 'husband' I keep hearing? (*She laughs hysterically.*) Is that what you want to be? You're no husband!

**Hudetz** (*shouting at her*) Enough! That's enough!

**Public Prosecutor** (*rising to his feet*) Enough of this squabbling! We're not here to discuss whether you're a husband or not, we're here, if you don't mind, because of a railway accident. And it's her word against yours. So I'm very sorry, Herr Hudetz, but because of your wife's incriminating statement, I'm obliged to take you into custody.

**Landlord** Custody?

**Public Prosecutor** (*gathering up his reports*) Everything will come to light at the trial – and if it turns out be a question of a spot of perjury . . .

*He glances at Frau Hudetz.*

**Frau Hudetz** (*uncannily calm*) Look at me as much as you like, sir, I'm not afraid of the light.

### SCENE THREE

*Four months have gone by. We're in the bar of the 'Savage' inn. In the background are the counter and two windows, on the left the outside door, on the right a door leading to the restaurant. On the wall is a picture of the 'savage' himself, with his beard and club and clothing made of pelts. Leni, the waitress, is up a ladder, pinning up a banner saying 'Welcome' over the door to the restaurant. Apart from this, the whole room is done out with Chinese lanterns and fir branches. At the moment, there's only one Customer, a truck driver, who is speedily scoffing his meal. It's autumn now, but the sun is still shining.*

**Customer** (*abruptly*) Where's my beer?

*Leni doesn't come down the ladder.*

**Leni** On its way!

*Silence.*

**Customer** (*dully menacing*) Are you going to bring me this fucking beer or aren't you?

**Leni** (*as before*) Just a minute!

*The Customer slams his fist down on the table.*

**Customer** (*yelling*) What do you think I am, stupid? I'm sitting down to eat and I still don't have any beer. I'm dying of thirst here, for Christ's sake, and you're pinning up decorations! Where's the sodding landlord?

*The Landlord has already come in from the left.*

**Landlord** I'm here. I'm very sorry, please don't take offence . . . (*He hectors Leni.*) Fetch the gentleman his beer immediately, what's come over you? You're making a pig's ear of this!

**Leni** (*dispiritedly*) But the banner . . .

**Landlord** (*cutting her off*) A customer is more important than a banner.

**Customer** Bloody right.

*Leni comes down the ladder, offended and draws a beer at the counter.*

**Landlord** Please, you must excuse us, we're a bit all over the place today, we're preparing this celebration party . . .

**Customer** (*pointing to the banner*) Who're you expecting, the Emperor of China?

**Landlord** (*smiling*) No, just one of our most admirable fellow citizens. You know that big railway accident four months ago?

**Customer** I'm a trucker, how should I know?

**Landlord** Well, at the time, our stationmaster was wrongly suspected, he suffered a bitter injustice. He's been on remand for four months, but yesterday afternoon he was totally rehabilitated – he walked free.

**Customer** Really? Fancy that, not many people walk free these days.

**Landlord** No, it's really inspiring, when the truth prevails and justice is seen to be done.

**Customer** Where's my beer?

**Leni** (*bringing it to him*) Here.

**Customer** I'll have the bill . . .

*He swallows the beer in one draught.*

**Leni** One set menu, one beer, four bread rolls – twenty-two.

**Customer** Not what you'd call a bargain . . .

*He throws the money on the table.*

**Leni** Thank you.

**Landlord** It's been a pleasure. Look forward to seeing you again!

**Customer** Not fucking likely.

*He goes out, left. The Landlord watches him go.*

**Landlord** (*melancholy*) There's some desperate people in the world . . .

*He turns to Leni, who's up the ladder again, and tries to look up her skirt without her noticing.*

People who just don't care. Not about anything – they don't care if someone walks free or gets out of jail, if they're innocent or guilty – all they can think about is beer.

**Leni** Everyone's stuck in their own groove.

**Landlord** You're right.

*Leni's fixed the banner.*

**Leni** There we are. That should stay up for ever.

*She comes down the ladder.*

What do you think Frau Hudetz is going to do now?

**Landlord** Her? She'd better never show her face round here – I think she'd get lynched, like them niggers in America.

**Leni** Take the Lord's name in vain, and He'll be down on you like a ton of bricks.

**Landlord** Saw how Anna kissed him, she did, with her own eyes. And she's also supposed to have seen him miss the signal and all. It was written all over her face she was lying, even the Public Prosecutor didn't believe a blind word of it, she'll be lucky if they don't do her for perjury. I'm telling you it's all over for Frau Hudetz. She's a thing of the past, she no longer exists. She'll be getting the divorce papers soon – goodbye, amen, over and out!

*Silence.*

**Leni** Do you think he'll get married again, the station-master?

**Landlord** Unless he's had enough of it. Why, is he up your street, old Hudetz?

**Leni** There's something about him.

**Landlord** (*paying attention*) How do you know?

**Leni** I just do.

*Silence.*

**Landlord** (*jokingly*) Who knows, perhaps he'll be leading you down the aisle.

*He grins. Leni looks at him, sadly.*

**Leni** I'm nothing special.

*Silence. The Landlord, regretting his sally, comes slowly up to her, gently puts his arm around her waist and begins to sing quietly, trying to cheer her up; but Leni remains unshakeably serious.*

**Landlord**
Don't be so hard-hearted, darling,
A girl isn't meant to be cold,

You know the old saying,
It's cooking and praying
And kindness to all, young and old.

*Ferdinand comes in quickly from the left.*
*The Landlord lets go of Leni, pleasantly surprised.*

Blimey, the prospective son-in-law! Hello, Ferdinand!

**Ferdinand**  Hello, Dad. Surprised to see me? I just nipped over on my motorbike, spur of the moment.

**Landlord**  Lot of work on?

**Ferdinand**  You said it! It was particularly tricky to get away today because of the cattle market.

**Landlord**  (*surprised*) Cattle market today?

**Ferdinand**  Certainly.

**Landlord**  They never used to have it on a Wednesday.

**Ferdinand**  (*disdainfully*) Some new regulation . . . (*Enthusiastically.*) Bulls they had, bulls the size of elephants – but I didn't let myself get side-tracked. The bull's not been born that'd be more important to me than Anna. Where is she?

**Leni**  Getting changed.

**Landlord**  (*to Leni*) Call her. Get a move on!

*Leni hurries off, right.*

I want to tell you something. Ferdinand, I'm very happy you've taken on my Anna, you'll run this place very well. Eighty-six years it's been in the family – don't forget that, when I'm no longer with you.

*Anna comes in, right, in a white dress.*

**Ferdinand**  Anna!

*He throws his arms round her and kisses her.*

36

**Anna** Nice surprise . . .

**Ferdinand** Since we saw each other last week, you've become a famous personality, star witness in a sensational court case. Look what they're calling you . . .

*He pulls a newspaper out of his pocket and shows her a headline.*

'The Innkeeper's Daughter, Pretty as a Picture' – in great big print.

**Landlord** She can be proud.

**Ferdinand** Me too.

**Anna** (*a strange smile*) Fame soon fades away.

**Landlord** Choice turn of phrase. My daughter knows how to put two words together.

**Ferdinand** No kidding, it's like being engaged to a film star! Let's have a look at you, star witness, see if you've changed at all . . .

*He looks her up and down.*

**Anna** (*another strange smile*) Very little.

*In the distance, the sound of military music, drawing closer. They all listen.*

**Ferdinand** Music?

**Landlord** They're on their way. They're on their way . . . (*He looks at his watch.*) It's them! Hudetz'll be here any minute – our Herr Hudetz! They've all turned out to meet him at the station, the whole town!

*Anna turns pale and puts a hand to her heart.*

**Ferdinand** What's the matter, Anna? Is it your little heart again?

**Anna** (*very quietly*) Yes.

**Landlord** (*to Ferdinand*) All this trial business has been a terrible strain on her.

**Ferdinand** (*stroking Anna's hand, tenderly*) It's all over now, though, isn't it, Anna?

**Anna** (*a forlorn smile*) Yes, it's all over now . . .

**Landlord** (*handing Anna a glass*) Have a drop of vermouth, nothing like it!

**Ferdinand** I'll have one too . . . (*He pours himself a glass. To Anna.*) Here's to you, Anna!

**Anna** (*tonelessly*) Here's to you, Ferdinand.

*They empty their glasses; and now the military music and cheers are close by. Leni bursts in excitedly, right; she's changed as well.*

**Leni** He's coming, he's coming, he's coming!

*She rushes over to the window, waves and shouts.*

Hooray!

*The Landlord and Ferdinand follow suit. The sun disappears, twilight falls fast. Anna is staring ahead of her; suddenly she pours herself another glass of vermouth.*

**Anna** (*tonelessly*) Hooray . . .

*She empties the glass. Now, the procession comes in the left-hand door, half the town is there, including, of course, Frau Leimgruber, the Woodsman and the Policeman, in dress uniform with white gloves. Hudetz steps in, smiling like a waxworks dummy, bowing gratefully in every direction; prison has turned him yellowish.*

**All** Hip, hip, hooray! Hip, hip, hooray! Hip, hip, hooray!

**Landlord** (*embarking on a speech*) Thomas Hudetz! Our dear friend! Our much respected stationmaster! All of us gathered here to greet you never lost our iron conviction that you were totally innocent – and it's a quite particular honour and personal pleasure to me that it was my daughter that fate decreed was to prove your innocence.

**Voices** Hooray for Anna, hooray!

**Landlord** There is a God in Heaven watching over us, so that the truth prevails and justice is seen to be done! Hail to you, innocent, who has had to go through so much suffering when they imprisoned you, an innocent man! Thomas Hudetz, our stationmaster, beloved by all – three cheers for our trusty friend!

*He goes up to Hudetz and shakes him by the hand.*

**All** Hip, hip, hooray! Hip, hip, hooray! Hip, hip, hooray!

*Music, a fanfare. A Child enters with a bouquet for Hudetz, curtsies and recites.*

**Child**
The song of the hero let us raise,
Let bells ring out and cymbals crash;
The man we gather here to praise
Acts for pure glory, not for cash.
Thank God, that I may ever raise
My voice in this brave hero's praise!

*The Child curtsies again and presents Hudetz with the bouquet.*
   *Everyone applauds.*
   *Hudetz caresses the Child's cheek, then suddenly becomes aware of Anna; he stops and stares at her, goes slowly over to her, offering her his hand.*

**Hudetz** Hello, Fräulein Anna.

**Anna** Hello, Herr Hudetz . . .

**Hudetz** How are you?

**Anna** Very well, thanks . . .

*She smiles. Everyone is watching Anna and Hudetz, curious to see what else they may say.*
*Hudetz becomes somewhat embarrassed, then, suddenly decisive, turns back to the crowd, pointing to Anna and speaking loudly.*

**Hudetz** My guardian angel! Three cheers for Anna!

*He hands over his bouquet. Everyone is beside themselves with enthusiasm.*

**All** Hip, hip, hooray! Hip, hip, hooray! Hip, hip, hooray!

*The lights are turned down in the restaurant and the band starts to play a waltz. The Landlord climbs up on a chair.*

**Landlord** Ladies and gentlemen, may I now request you to move into the restaurant? I imagine you're all ravenous and dying of thirst, and anyway it seems to have got dark in here!

*Laughter and applause. Ferdinand offers Anna his arm.*

**Ferdinand** May I . . . ?

*Everyone leaves in a celebratory mood, except for Leni.*
*Leni stands behind the counter, drawing off several glasses of beer and humming the waltz tune that's playing in the restaurant.*
*Alfons comes in, left.*
*Leni sees him, starts and stares at him, horrified.*

**Alfons** Good evening, Leni. Why are you looking at me like that?

**Leni** I don't know how you dare come here.

**Alfons** (*smiling*) Why shouldn't I?

**Leni** Well, your sister, Frau Hudetz . . .

**Alfons** (*interrupting her*) I have no sister. Not any more.

**Leni** No one's going to believe that. Careful – they'll throw you out on your ear!

*Alfons sits down.*

(*Anxiously.*) Why don't you go, they'll beat you up, they'll have a few drinks and they'll kick your head in.

**Alfons** (*smiling*) Let them . . .

**Leni** (*annoyed*) If you won't listen, there's nothing I can do for you.

*She heads off, right, with several tankards of beer.*
 *In the restaurant, a woman singer is singing 'Der Lenz ist da' by Hildach.*

**Singer** (*offstage*)
 The finches carol
 The spring is here!
 It came out of nowhere
 Like every year.

 It stole up upon us
 All in one night
 In all its old glory
 So shining bright.

 The spring waters ripple
 The breezes blow
 The sky is cloudless
 The buds swell and grow.

 So ring out the church bells
 Far and near
 And start your rejoicing
 The spring is here!

*Alfons listens to the song, gets up, moves slowly towards the restaurant, then comes to a halt, hesitating.*

*The singer comes to an end, enthusiastic applause and cheers.*

*Alfons is taken aback by the sheer volume of the delighted response; he quickly puts on his hat and leaves, left.*

*Silence.*

*Anna comes in hurriedly, right, with Hudetz. They talk quickly, they seem oppressed. She has an exploratory look round, anxious.*

**Anna**  No one'll see us here.

**Hudetz**  What is it you want from me?

**Anna**  I need to talk to you.

**Hudetz**  Can't you do that in the restaurant?

**Anna**  No, everyone's looking at us in there – Herr Hudetz, I have to talk to you tomorrow, just the two of us, there's something I have to tell you . . .

**Hudetz**  What do you have to tell me?

**Anna**  (*smiling*) Oh, there's so much to say!

*Silence.*

**Hudetz**  It'd be much better for us not to see each other.

**Anna**  No, it's all right, it'll be all right – I'm going under . . .

*She smiles.*

**Hudetz**  Quiet!

*He looks around carefully. Silence.*

We have to go back in. What would your fiancé think, if he saw us here? He'd think there was something between us and that'd just be the last straw.

42

**Anna** Herr Hudetz, please have pity on me. You have to listen to what I have to say tomorrow.

**Hudetz** You're talking as if your life depended on it.

**Anna** Maybe it does . . .

*She smiles. Silence.*

**Hudetz** All right, then, tomorrow. Where?

**Anna** By the viaduct.

**Hudetz** On top or below?

**Anna** Below.

**Hudetz** When?

**Anna** Nine o'clock in the evening.

**Hudetz** Nine o'clock? That's the middle of the night.

**Anna** (*smiling*) Then no one'll see us. At least no one human.

**Hudetz** (*shrugging his shoulders*) All right.

**Anna** (*holding out her hand*) Agreed then?

**Hudetz** (*taking it*) Agreed.

**Anna** (*smiling*) Good.

*She hurries off, right.*
*Another waltz plays in the restaurant.*
*Alfons returns, left, sees Hudetz and clutches at his heart.*

**Hudetz** (*staring at him, quietly*) Is that you, Alfons?

**Alfons** Yes.

*Pause.*

**Hudetz** (*grinning*) Evening, brother-in-law.

**Alfons** Good evening, Thomas. Don't say 'brother-in-law' in that sarcastic way – a woman who behaves the way my sister has doesn't exist for me any more.

**Hudetz** Never mind. It's all in the past.

**Alfons** Not for me.

*Hudetz looks at him. Pause.*

I was here earlier, but I was told my head was going to be kicked in . . .

*He grins, then abruptly turns serious.*

I'm not afraid of anything any more. I've worked it all out. There's only one course open to me: to make a public announcement that I've broken with my sister. It's over between me and her. I can't go on like this. I say good morning and nobody answers. I'm used to being boycotted, but now they want to run me into the ground. Thomas, we've never had a quarrel. Please, help me . . .

*The Landlord, Frau Leimgruber, Ferdinand, Anna and the Woodsman come in from the restaurant.*
*The Landlord turns the light on and sees Hudetz.*

**Landlord** There you are, we've been looking for you . . .

*He breaks off, having noticed Alfons.*

**Landlord** Hah! What's this? You dare show your face here? I've never heard of such impertinence! Out!

**Frau Leimgruber** Out! Get out of here!

**Alfons** No! I have something to say to you . . .

**Landlord** (*rudely interrupting him*) There's nothing you can say to us! Get out, now, or I can't be responsible for what happens.

**Woodsman** (*approaching Alfons*) Quack, perjurer . . .

*He's about to get physical.*

44

**Hudetz** Stop! He's just explained to me that he's broken with his sister . . .

**Ferdinand** He's lying.

**Hudetz** (*sharply*) He is not lying!

**Landlord** (*baffled, to Hudetz*) That it should be you of all people . . .

**Hudetz** That's right. Do me a favour and leave him in peace.

*He goes out, right.*

### SCENE FOUR

*The foot of a canyon; the pillars of the viaduct tower up towards the sky. It's a lonely night. The moon is shining, autumn's coming on, everything's as silent as the grave. The Policeman is doing his rounds. He stops suddenly and peers into the darkness.*

**Policeman** Is there someone there? Hello! Who's there?

**Hudetz** (*stepping forward*) Evening, Inspector . . .

**Policeman** (*reassured*) Oh, it's the stationmaster. What are you doing out here by the viaduct?

**Hudetz** Just out for a walk.

**Policeman** In the middle of the night?

**Hudetz** I don't mind the dark . . .

*He smiles.*

**Policeman** You be careful, there's all kinds of riff-raff lurking about round here, I just had an official report about it. Gypsies, I think.

**Hudetz** (*cutting him off*) Doesn't worry me.

**Policeman** (*smiling*) Ah, yes, 'a quiet conscience sleeps in thunder' – how much time off have they given you, Herr Hudetz?

**Hudetz** A week.

**Policeman** Is that all? You'd better not go to too many parties like last night's – my God, it went on and on! Till six in the morning!

**Hudetz** It was fun.

**Policeman** And the drink, life-threatening amounts of drink there were! How late did you sleep today?

**Hudetz** I didn't sleep. I haven't been sleeping very well lately.

**Policeman** I know what it's like. I don't sleep so well myself. You lie there in the dark and all sorts of things go through your head – all the ways you could have done better.

**Hudetz** That as well.

**Policeman** Well, goodnight, Herr Hudetz. Hope you have a good rest.

*He salutes and moves off.*

**Hudetz** Goodnight, Inspector.

*He looks around, then lights a cigarette; up on the viaduct a signal bell rings, like the signal bell in the station. He listens, looking upwards. Anna arrives, sees him and starts visibly.*

Did I scare you?

**Anna** (*smiling*) You appeared out of nowhere . . .

*The church clock strikes in the distant town. Hudetz quietly counts the number of strokes.*

**Hudetz** . . . Nine – I've been here since quarter to . . . (*He grins.*) You don't keep a lady waiting.

*Silence.*

**Anna** (*looking around carefully*) I crept out, I don't want anyone to know we're meeting.

**Hudetz** Couldn't agree more.

**Anna** People would only talk and there's no reason for that, is there?

**Hudetz** Not that I know of.

*High above them, a train travels across the viaduct.*

**Anna** (*looking up*) The stopping train . . .

**Hudetz** (*also looking upwards*) No, that's the express.

**Anna** It's going so slowly, made me think . . .

**Hudetz** Yes, it's deceptive.

**Anna** It is.

*Silence.*

**Hudetz** What was it you wanted to tell me?

**Anna** A lot of things. Really, a lot of things.

**Hudetz** One at a time, then. First, second, third.

*Silence.*

**Anna** Have you stopped hearing voices in your head, Herr Hudetz?

*Hudetz stares at her.*

What would you say if I was to shout out that I was lying, that I perjured myself, that the signal was . . .

**Hudetz** (*shouting her down*) Be quiet!

*He looks around.*
*Silence.*

**Anna** (*quietly, but urgently*) What would you do, Herr Hudetz?

**Hudetz** I, erm, I really don't know.

**Anna** That's not true.

**Hudetz** What do you think I'd do?

**Anna** I know what you'd do.

*Silence.*

**Hudetz** I wouldn't kill you.

**Anna** (*smiling*) Pity.

*Hudetz is surprised.*
*Silence.*

(*Very simply.*) I don't want to go on living, Herr Hudetz.

**Hudetz** It was your duty to swear that oath the way you did, you had no choice.

**Anna** (*letting fly at him*) You're wrong if you think it was all my fault, I'm not having that, oh, no!

**Hudetz** Then whose fault was it?

**Anna** Not mine, not all mine!

**Hudetz** (*sarcastically, like the Public Prosecutor*) Who else then? A person or persons unknown?

**Anna** Maybe.

*Up on the viaduct, the signal bell rings again. Hudetz looks upwards.*

(*Frightened.*) What was that?

**Hudetz** The signal.

*Anna suddenly puts her hands over her ears.*

**Anna** (*quietly*) I keep hearing that wailing – I can't bear being alone, Herr Hudetz, the ghosts come, they're angry with me, they want to fetch me away . . .

*Silence.*

**Hudetz** Listen, I've been on my own for four months, in solitary confinement, no one's company but my own, so I had plenty of opportunity to listen to my inner voices, every hour of the day. We had good long conversations, Fräulein Anna – and you know what my inner voice said to me? 'You've always followed orders and done your duty,' it said. 'You've never missed a signal in your life, dear Thomas, you're innocent . . .'

**Anna** (*interrupting him*) Innocent?

**Hudetz** Completely.

**Anna** (*letting fly at him*) Aren't you making it a bit too easy on yourself?

**Hudetz** (*shouting at her*) I'm not making it too easy on myself, the only thing I did wrong was not to chase you off right away, that I was so polite to you, when I should have given you a good smack, all right?

*Silence.*

**Anna** (*smiling*) You should have given me a good smack?

**Hudetz** Yes.

*Silence.*

**Anna** Pity you didn't . . .

**Hudetz** Yes, I'm sorry, as well.

**Anna** Why don't you give me a good smack right now? Perhaps it'd do the trick.

**Hudetz** (*shouting at her again*) This is no time to make stupid jokes!

**Anna** It's not a joke. Then it was, when I kissed you . . .

**Hudetz** (*interrupting her*) Don't keep talking about that!

**Anna** (*smiling*) I don't know what else to talk about . . .

**Hudetz** Then you'd better shut up, or there'll be another accident!

*Silence.*

**Anna** How do you mean, Herr Hudetz?

**Hudetz** What?

**Anna** What sort of accident?

*Silence.*

**Hudetz** (*staring at her*) I walked free, Fräulein Anna, gloriously free.

**Anna** Then maybe you'll have to do something even more serious, so that you can be properly punished . . .

*A gentle smile.*
*Silence.*

**Hudetz** (*letting fly at her*) Don't look at me like that!

**Anna** (*smiling*) Are you afraid? Of me?

**Hudetz** (*staring at her*) You're white as a sheet . . .

**Anna** It's the moon, Herr Hudetz, that's all . . .

**Hudetz** (*as before*) As if there wasn't a drop of blood in your body, not a drop . . .

**Anna** Oh, there's enough!

*She laughs.*

**Hudetz** (*shouting her down*) Stop it!

*Silence.*

I'm going.

**Anna** Where?

**Hudetz** To sleep.

**Anna** Can you sleep?

**Hudetz** Yes.

*He starts to go.*

**Anna** Wait! Herr Hudetz, my life changed, quite suddenly. At first I thought nothing of it, but now everything is different and when night falls, the stars catch me by surprise. Our house has got smaller, Herr Hudetz, and as for Ferdinand, I look at him quite differently now – they're all like strangers to me now – my father, Leni, all of them, every one of them – except you, Herr Hudetz. When you arrived yesterday, I already knew what you were going to look like, your nose, your eyes, your chin, your ears – as if I remembered you, even though we've never taken much notice of one another in the past – but now I know every inch of you. Is that the way you feel about me?

**Hudetz** (*without turning back to her, after a short pause*) Yes.

**Anna** (*smiling gently*) Good!

*Silence.*

If I was to die, Herr Hudetz, I'd still belong to you – we'll never stop seeing each other . . .

*Hudetz goes slowly up to her, slowly lifts her chin and looks into her eyes, as if he were quietly calling to her.*

**Hudetz** Anna, Anna . . .

**Anna** (*very quietly*) Now do you recognise me?

**Hudetz** Yes . . .

*He kisses her and she puts her arms around him.*


### SCENE FIVE

*Three days later, back in the 'Savage' inn. The welcome sign, the Chinese lanterns and the fir branches have disappeared. It's raining outside. Leni leans over a table, reading the newspaper. Hudetz comes in, left.*

**Leni** Evening, Herr Hudetz.

**Hudetz** Small carafe of red . . .

*He sits down.*

**Leni** Since when are you drinking red wine?

**Hudetz** Since today.

**Leni** Strange.

*She pours the wine out.*
*Silence.*

**Hudetz** Any developments?

**Leni** (*bringing him the wine*) Still nothing. They're groping in the dark.

**Hudetz** Mmm.

*He drinks.*

**Leni** It's three days tonight since Anna disappeared – disappeared, as if the earth swallowed her up. I was the last to see her – she said she was going to bed, she was exhausted after the party, but the next morning her bed was untouched, totally untouched . . .

**Hudetz** Mmm.

**Leni** Her father offered a reward today for any useful information – he and Herr Ferdinand had a long discussion yesterday about the amount he should offer. I hope she hasn't been kidnapped by white slave traders or anything like that . . .

**Hudetz** Old wives' tales.

**Leni** I don't like to say it out loud, Herr Hudetz, but I don't think she's alive . . .

*She breaks off and, suddenly interested, inspects his cheek.*

What's that?

**Hudetz** What?

**Leni** (*teasingly*) Who's scratched you then?

**Hudetz** Nobody. Did it myself. On a rusty nail . . .

*He grins. Leni points at him.*

**Leni** (*teasingly*) Oh yes? I can think what I like, they can't charge you for it.

*She's wiping glasses.*

By the way, guess who's been back in town since yesterday evening? Your wife.

**Hudetz** (*puzzled*) Who?

**Leni** Your wife, the one you're divorcing . . .

**Hudetz** (*cutting her off*) Oh, her!

**Leni** She's living at the chemist's, with her brother – the very chemist who made a public statement that he no longer had a sister and who you defended. What have you got to say to that?

53

**Hudetz** (*grinning grimly*) Better keep my mouth shut from now on.

**Leni** And you know what people are saying? No one's criticising, they think it's all perfectly normal. That's right, ever since Anna disappeared, the chemist's turned into Almighty God – all of a sudden, every time he's mentioned, it's with the greatest respect. People are so fickle!

*The church clock strikes.*

**Hudetz** The hell with people! (*He counts tonelessly.*) Six.

**Leni** Six o'clock already. Time slips away . . .

**Hudetz** Yes.

*He drinks, then speaks with deliberate casualness, as if by the way.*

What makes you think Fräulein Anna isn't alive?

*Leni looks around carefully and leans over close to him.*

**Leni** (*quietly*) She's done away with herself, I could swear to it . . .

*Hudetz is staring at her.*
*Leni meets his gaze.*

You understand what I'm saying, Herr Hudetz?

**Hudetz** (*momentarily confused*) Me? Why? What are you getting at?

**Leni** (*as before*) Haven't you heard?

**Hudetz** Heard what? What's it to do with me? Spit it out!

**Leni** You won't be angry with me . . .?

**Hudetz** I won't be angry with you, now come on!

*Leni looks around carefully again and speaks even more quietly than before.*

**Leni** Since poor Anna has disappeared, people have stopped believing her – they're even saying it wouldn't be such a terrible thing for Herr Hudetz if Fräulein Anna wasn't around to talk any more . . .

*Hudetz is staring at her.*

They're saying, Anna chose death, because the voices in her head gave her no peace.

**Hudetz** (*as before*) Voices in her head?

**Leni** People think Anna lied under oath, perjured herself, because . . .

*She breaks off.*

**Hudetz** (*urgently*) Because?

**Leni** Because, Herr Hudetz, you didn't set the signal in time . . .

*Silence.*
*Hudetz laughs, then suddenly looks serious again.*
*Silence.*

What are you going to do, Herr Hudetz?

**Hudetz** I did set the signal in time. I've always followed orders and done my duty . . .

*He drinks.*
*The Policeman comes in, left; he looks very serious.*

**Leni** Evening, Inspector.

**Policeman** Is the landlord in?

**Leni** Yes.

**Policeman** I need to speak to him immediately.

**Leni** (*alarmed*) For goodness' sake, what's happened?

**Policeman** We found Anna. Dead.

**Leni** Jesus, Mary and Joseph! (*She crosses herself.*) So she did do away with herself.

**Policeman** No, she didn't do away with herself, she's been murdered.

**Leni** Murdered . . .

**Policeman** We're already following a particular lead. She was found out by the viaduct, beneath it, and we've had a report, all kinds of riff-raff lurking about round there, gypsies . . . (*To Hudetz.*) I think I told you, Herr Hudetz –

**Hudetz** Right.

**Policeman** That was that same night, when we met out by the viaduct, beneath it . . .

**Hudetz** Right.

**Policeman** Tell me, Herr Hudetz, you didn't notice anything suspicious out there, did you?

**Hudetz** No.

**Policeman** Hmm.

*He looks closely at Hudetz.*

Though the mills of God grind slowly . . .

**Hudetz** I didn't see any gypsies.

**Policeman** She wasn't murdered by gypsies – goodbye, Herr Hudetz.

**Hudetz** Goodbye.

*The Policeman goes out, right.*
*Silence.*

**Leni** (*staring at him*) So you were out by the viaduct that night?

**Hudetz** Yes.

*He gets up.*

**Leni** Are you going already?

**Hudetz** Bill, please.

**Leni** (*suddenly shouts at him*) What were you doing out by the viaduct?

**Hudetz** Me? (*He smiles.*) I was getting engaged to Fräulein Anna . . .

*He salutes and goes quickly out, left.*


SCENE SIX

*At the chemist's, three days later. A desk in the background, a small table and two chairs, downstage left. On the right, the entrance door and part of the window display as seen from the inside; on the left, a concealed door leading to the living quarters. It's late in the afternoon, just before closing time.*

**Frau Leimgruber** It's a real shame you weren't at the poor child's funeral, it was really something! People came from near and far, even more people than what turned up after the railway disaster, all the newspaper reporters, and they photographed the grave for the *People's Illustrated* from every angle you can think of! And there were flowers – you've never seen so many flowers! You really missed something. Of course I sympathise completely, your not wanting to accompany poor Annie on her final journey, when it was your former brother-in-law who – I quite understand – I quite understand! It was very tactful, very tactful indeed! Just a minute, what are you doing? That's much too big for me to carry, can't you make it two parcels?

**Alfons** If you like . . .

**Frau Leimgruber** It'd be nice, you know, her father, poor devil, he was bent double with grief, but very contained, whereas Ferdinand, the fiancé, well, he broke down completely, he was absolutely in shreds – tears pouring down his face, broke your heart. No, you wouldn't credit the amount of tender feelings hidden away in that great lump of a butcher, and vice versa. I'm telling you, often as not, a child's heart beats in the most savage breast. Poor little Annie! You're in your grave now, on your own, no one to tuck you in when it rains. Here's the picture, look, they took of her when she was laid out, they put it on the memorial booklet – I'll leave you one, shall I, I've got a whole stack of them . . .

*She leaves one on the desk.*

**Alfons** (*without looking up*) Thank you, Frau Leimgruber.

*Silence.*

**Frau Leimgruber** And how's your sister? Her health good?

**Alfons** (*smiling*) Well, she's . . .

**Frau Leimgruber** Of course, of course! She's had so much excitement, but if I were her, I'd be grateful he hadn't done me in – which he could easily have done. I was thinking today, all the way through that tragic ceremony, how very satisfying it must be for her that they're on his tail, that upstanding stationmaster, that Hudetz, that gangster – hope they catch him soon. I must tell you, I'm so happy there's been this thaw in relations, everybody speaks about you and your poor sister with total respect, as if they're all feeling a tiny bit ashamed . . .

**Alfons** No shame in feeling ashamed. But I'd like to say one thing: none of this gives me any satisfaction. I'd rather the terrible deed had never been committed.

**Frau Leimgruber** Get on with you, really! That's just a bit too high-minded! Careful you don't finish up acting too noble or they'll turn against you again.

**Alfons** I'm only saying what I genuinely believe.

**Frau Leimgruber** Doesn't mean it's the truth, though, does it?

**Alfons** My sister was spat at, when she told the truth.

**Frau Leimgruber** But that was a mistake, a terrible mistake! Whereas there are no mistakes in this Thomas Hudetz business. Hudetz seduced poor Annie into committing perjury, it was his criminal influence, nothing else, and when she broke down, and her guilty conscience made her repent and want to confess everything, he simply did away with her – and it wasn't her kissed him at the station, he's the one who kissed her and it wasn't just a kiss, he tried to rape her in his office and she fell on to the signal lever . . .

**Alfons** (*interrupting her angrily*) How do you know all this? Were you there?

**Frau Leimgruber** I beg your pardon?

**Alfons** I'm not going to put up with this! What I say is, as long as it's not been proved beyond the shadow of a doubt that he's the killer, as long as he hasn't confessed to it, freely confessed to it himself, he's not guilty as far as I'm concerned, I refuse to believe it.

**Frau Leimgruber** Seems to me, you're the type refuses to believe in anything. God, anything.

**Alfons** Do I need you to talk to me about God? Hudetz is not the worst person round here, let me tell you, not by a long chalk, Frau Leimgruber.

**Frau Leimgruber** (*very sharply*) Oh, I see, now we're being compared with murderers.

**Alfons** Just remember how he protected me when you wanted me beaten up.

**Frau Leimgruber** (*vindictively*) Perhaps it would have been better if he hadn't protected you! My goodness, it's really impossible to have any sort of normal conversation with you – it just can't be done!

*She snatches her two parcels out of his hand and leaves quickly, right. Alfons is alone. He smiles, silent, and holds a hand in front of his eyes. The church clock strikes seven. He checks his watch.*

**Alfons** That's it. Another day gone . . .

*He goes slowly out of the entrance door and he can be heard rolling down the iron shutters on the shop windows.*

*Frau Hudetz comes in through the concealed door with supper on a tray. She lays the table.*

*Alfons reappears through the entrance door, closing it behind him; then he sits at the small table and eats.*

*Frau Hudetz has already sat down and started eating.*

**Frau Hudetz** (*abruptly*) You've been talking to the customers about him again, haven't you?

**Alfons** Yes.

**Frau Hudetz** I could hear you from the kitchen, not everything you were saying, but you were defending him again, weren't you?

**Alfons**  Yes.

*Silence.*

**Frau Hudetz**  Why can't we eat in the other room? It stinks of chemicals in here.

**Alfons**  We'd have to heat the other room.

**Frau Hudetz**  (*smiles somewhat sarcastically*) I never knew you were stingy . . .

**Alfons**  If I weren't stingy, you wouldn't be going to the seaside.

*Silence.*

**Frau Hudetz**  Then we'll eat in the kitchen tomorrow.

**Alfons**  I've never eaten in the kitchen before, but just as you like.

*Silence.*

**Frau Hudetz**  Taste all right?

**Alfons**  Fine.

*Silence.*

**Frau Hudetz**  What would you like tomorrow?

**Alfons**  Whatever you're making.

*Suddenly Frau Hudetz stops eating and puts her knife and fork down next to her plate.*

**Frau Hudetz**  Sometimes I wonder whose crimes we're having to atone for . . .

**Alfons**  Our own.

**Frau Hudetz**  No, not me . . .

**Alfons**  Oh, yes.

**Frau Hudetz** I'm not aware of having committed any crimes.

**Alfons** Doesn't make any difference. You've just forgotten them.

**Frau Hudetz** (*sharply*) Is that what you think?

**Alfons** I genuinely believe it.

**Frau Hudetz** Doesn't mean it's the truth, though, does it?

**Alfons** You sound like Frau Leimgruber.

**Frau Hudetz** (*very sharply*) Oh, I see, now we're being compared with slanderers . . .

**Alfons** (*smiling*) Exactly like Leimgruber!

*Frau Hudetz stares at him coldly, then shrugs her shoulders.*

**Frau Hudetz** I'm innocent.

**Alfons** Innocent!

*He laughs.*

**Frau Hudetz** (*shouting at him*) Don't laugh! Tell me one thing I've done wrong, one single crime I've committed!

*Alfons gets up and paces up and down.*

**Alfons** I remember you said to me, 'If Thomas doesn't want me any more, I'll make sure he never looks at another woman, never!' You had no right to say that, that was a crime!

**Frau Hudetz** (*scornfully*) That's a crime I'll own up to.

**Alfons** Then don't complain when you're punished for it. Don't accuse people of persecuting you. You were thirteen years older, you must have known it, you must have felt it – but you wanted to hold his love by blackmailing him, that's right, blackmailing him!

**Frau Hudetz** Stop shouting. What do you know about women? None of them ever comes near you . . .

**Alfons** (*staring at her*) Didn't you say to me, 'I hate him, that's right I hate him, and when he's lying next to me at night, I could easily kill him . . .' (*He lets fly at her.*) Did you or did you not say that?

**Frau Hudetz** (*uncannily calm*) I did. But I didn't kill him, did I?

*She grins.*

**Alfons** Maybe not.

*Silence.*

**Frau Hudetz** The way you're talking, it was me that missed the signal, it was me that killed those eighteen people.

**Alfons** (*cutting her off*) It's all connected.

**Frau Hudetz** (*suddenly screaming at him*) And Anna, I suppose it was me, was it, I suppose I . . .

*There is a knock on the outside door.*
*Both of them start and listen.*

(*Anxiously.*) Who's that?

*Another knock. Alfons turns towards the entrance.*

**Alfons** Let's have a look . . .

**Frau Hudetz** Be careful, Alfons.

*Alfons opens the outside door and shrinks back.*

**Alfons** (*stifled*) You?

*Hudetz steps in. His uniform is crumpled, he's lost his cap.*

**Frau Hudetz** (*a stifled cry*) Thomas!

*Alfons quickly closes the outside door.*

*Hudetz doesn't even look at them, he crosses slowly to the small table, contemplates what's left of the food, eventually takes a bread roll and eats apathetically. The others stare at him.*

*Hudetz stops eating, looks at them both and smiles.*

**Hudetz**  How are you?

**Frau Hudetz**  Thomas, have you taken leave of your senses?

**Hudetz**  (*shouting at her*) Be quiet! Stop shouting!

*He looks around, suspicious.*

**Alfons**  Are they after you?

**Hudetz**  (*grinning*) Of course.

*Silence.*

**Alfons**  What do you want from us?

**Hudetz**  I've been hiding in the woods until today, then I crept over here . . .

*He grins.*

Don't worry. Nobody saw me . . . (*He becomes serious, matter-of-fact.*) I need a suit, civvies. I have to get away and I can't do that in uniform.

*Silence.*

So will you give me a suit or won't you?

**Frau Hudetz**  (*letting fly at him*) Why do you have to get us involved? That would be aiding and abetting. Leave my brother out of this; and you've caused me enough misery. Leave us in peace!

**Hudetz**  (*grinning again*) Oh, you're in peace, are you?

*Silence.*

64

**Alfons** We're trying to be. And trying to do the right thing.

**Hudetz** You are perhaps . . .

**Alfons** (*shouting at him*) Don't talk to us like this! Look into your heart!

*Silence.*

**Hudetz** (*grinning*) What do you want me to do? Look into my heart? What am I supposed to find?

**Alfons** Just look.

*Hudetz listens out for something and stops grinning. Silence.*

**Hudetz** The whole area's swarming with police and military. But I can get through. I'm not going to go to jail. I don't deserve to, it's not my fault.

**Alfons** Is that what you think?

**Hudetz** I'm innocent.

**Frau Hudetz** (*laughing hysterically*) You're like Frau Leimgruber, just like Frau Leimgruber!

**Hudetz** Don't laugh.

**Frau Hudetz** It's too funny, it really is . . .

*She sits down at the small table, bends over the plates and bursts into tears.*

**Hudetz** (*to Alfons*) What's the matter with her?

*Silence.*

**Alfons** Thomas, I really didn't want to believe that you . . .

**Hudetz** That I what? Ah! – Well, I can't help you, you'll have to believe it – I got engaged to Anna.

**Frau Hudetz** (*horrified*) Engaged?

**Hudetz** (*nodding*) Out by the viaduct. Mmm . . .

*He smiles.*

I grabbed hold of her and shook her, but she wasn't there any more – I called out to her but she didn't make a sound. Then I went home and lay down. Suddenly, after four months, I was able to sleep again, like a man who's always followed orders and done his duty . . .

*He smiles.*

Well.

*He thinks for a moment and slowly takes his head in his hands.*

Yes, there's something I wanted to ask you. I know I killed her, but I don't know how – how?

*He looks at Alfons and Frau Hudetz.*

How did I do it?

*Both of them are staring at him, appalled.*

Did you read anything about it in the paper?

**Alfons** No, we didn't want to read about it.

**Hudetz** If only I knew the answer . . .

**Alfons** Then what?

**Hudetz** Well, then – yes, then I'd know myself, know myself a little better . . .

*Silence.*

(*To Frau Hudetz.*) You know I always defended you?

**Frau Hudetz** Yes. But when you were with me, you were always thinking of somebody else . . .

66

**Hudetz** (*nodding and smiling*) The girl I was engaged to . . .

**Frau Hudetz** Oh, Thomas! Don't let's talk about it any more, I'm so tired.

**Hudetz** Me too. But I have a long way to go . . .

**Alfons** (*to Frau Hudetz*) Fetch him my grey suit. Come on.

**Frau Hudetz** (*to Alfons*) He's going to get you into trouble.

**Alfons** Go on.

*Frau Hudetz goes out by the concealed door.*
*Silence.*

**Hudetz** Somebody said to me, 'You walked free and now you'll have to commit an even more serious crime, so that you can be properly punished . . .'

*He holds a hand in front of his eyes.*

Who was it said that – who?

**Alfons** Was it Anna?

*Hudetz starts and stares at Alfons in amazement.*

**Hudetz** Yes. How did you know?

**Alfons** Well, I wasn't there . . .

*He smiles.*
*Silence.*

**Hudetz** (*staring at Alfons*) No. Neither was I.

*He smiles; he finds the memorial booklet on the desk.*

What's this? (*He reads out.*) 'In reverent memory of a highly esteemed innocent young woman, Anna Lechner, an innkeeper's daughter of this parish . . .' (*To Alfons.*) Was it a beautiful funeral?

**Alfons**  It was.

*Hudetz smiles gently and happily and contemplates the photograph a little longer. Then, his expression serious, he turns it over and reads, as if he were simply reading it out to somebody.*

**Hudetz**
'Wanderer, stand still, take pause,
Think of the pain my wounds did cause,
Time slips away
The pain doth stay
And if thou hast transgressed my laws
Be on your guard, beware, I say,
Of Judgment Day . . .'

*Frau Hudetz comes back with the grey suit and lays it across a chair.*

**Frau Hudetz**  (*to Hudetz, who's lost in contemplation*)
You should go now, Thomas . . .

**Hudetz**  (*as if to himself*)  Yes.

*He turns towards the outside door.*

**Frau Hudetz**  What about the suit?

*Hudetz glances at the suit, then looks straight at both of them.*

**Hudetz**  (*smiling*)  No, thanks – it's all right . . .

*He leaves through the entrance door.*


### SCENE SEVEN

*On the embankment, where once express train 405 collided with a goods train. The middle of the night, and the signal is set at green for go. The Policeman, with his*

*fixed bayonet, comes on, right, followed by the Landlord
and Ferdinand, armed with their hunting rifles. They're
moving left; then the Landlord stops suddenly and listens
in the darkness.*

**Landlord** There's someone there – Hello! Who's there?

*Silence.*

**Policeman** It's nothing. Often it's just the night you hear.

**Landlord** (*grimly*) He's going to get away . . .

**Policeman** No chance, I guarantee it. The entire
neighbourhood's on full alert, we've got him surrounded.

**Ferdinand** (*suddenly sobbing sentimentally*) Oh, my
Annie, poor little Annie – where are you now?

**Policeman** In Paradise.

**Ferdinand** What good is that to me . . .?

*He pulls out a bottle and drinks.*

**Landlord** (*discreetly*) You shouldn't drink so much.

**Ferdinand** Reason I'm drinking, I should have protected
her, my friends – oh, Annie, Annie, I'm a bad person, I'm
a miserable wretch.

**Landlord** Get a grip.

**Ferdinand** (*shouting at the Landlord*) I don't want to get
a grip. It's all right for you, you were only her father, but
I was her fiancé and she was the love of my life, if it's all
the same to you.

*He drinks some more.*
    *Alfons appears from the right, sees the three of them
and stops.*
    *The three of them see him and stare at him,
transfixed.*

**Alfons**  Good evening.

*Silence.*
*The Landlord is the first to find his voice.*

**Landlord**  You dare show your face to me . . .?

**Alfons**  (*cutting him off*) Yes. (*To the Policeman.*) I was looking for you, Inspector.

**Policeman**  Where's your brother-in-law?

**Alfons**  (*smiling somewhat uncertainly*) Oh, you already know . . .

**Policeman**  (*puzzled*) Know what?

**Landlord**  Look at the way he's smiling . . .

*He stares vindictively at Alfons.*

**Alfons**  Well, my brother-in-law, Thomas Hudetz, came to see me this evening . . .

**Ferdinand**  (*cutting him off*) Came to see you?

**Alfons**  Unexpectedly.

**Landlord**  (*sarcastically*) Unexpectedly?

**Alfons**  Yes. (*To the Policeman.*) He came to see me and asked for a change of clothes, a suit . . .

**Policeman**  (*cutting him off, harshly*) And? You gave him a suit, did you?

**Alfons**  (*after a short pause*) He thought better of it . . . (*He smiles.*) Yes, he decided not to take it. And I came to a decision too, Inspector, about whether to report what happened, since he'd come to me for help; and I think it has to be reported – in his own interest, as much as anything else.

**Ferdinand**  He has no interest and don't you forget it!

**Landlord** So where's he hiding, your brother-in-law? Where is he, our much-loved stationmaster?

**Alfons** When he left me, I followed him – but then I lost track of him. He was heading for the viaduct.

**Landlord** The viaduct?

*He clutches at his heart.*

**Alfons** Yes. God help him.

*Silence.*

Do you understand now, why he didn't want to take the suit?

**Policeman** Why?

**Alfons** A viaduct is generally very high . . .

*A strange smile.*
*Silence.*

**Policeman** Oh, you mean he's going to jump off?

**Ferdinand** Jump off?

**Alfons** I'm afraid he's judged himself . . .

**Landlord** Judged himself? Well, that's not good enough. I'm not having that! That'd be too easy. What's he think he's doing? Kill my child, my only child and then just simply . . .? No, that's just too easy!

**Ferdinand** He's got to be locked up and beheaded. Off with his head, off with his head.

**Policeman** A proper legal process . . .

**Landlord** (*cutting him off*) I'm going to find him. Let's go to the viaduct!

*He hurries off, left.*

**Ferdinand** I'm going to find him as well – come on, Inspector! (*To Alfons.*) And you can go to bed.

*He hurries off, left.*

**Alfons** No, I'm going to find him as well. He shall not escape from judgment on this earth.

**Policeman** Well said!

*He hurries off with Alfons, left.*
*Pokorny, the dead engine driver, steps out of the darkness, smoking a Virginian cigarette; he watches Alfons leave and grins.*

**Pokorny** Judgment on this earth, bloody idiot!

*The signal bell rings and the signal changes to red.*
*A Platelayer appears on the embankment; he's carrying a lamp attached to his chest, so that his face is not visible.*

(*Quietly.*) How are you, Kreitmeyer?

*The Platelayer stops, his voice is soft.*

**Platelayer** My respects, Herr Pokorny.

**Pokorny** Where is he?

**Platelayer** Up at the viaduct.

**Pokorny** Has he jumped yet?

**Platelayer** No. Seems nervous . . .

**Pokorny** Nervous? I'll have to have another word with him.

**Platelayer** (*anxiously*) Don't do that.

**Pokorny** I certainly will. Even if it costs me a thousand years – cheap at the price! You died as well, didn't you? You were on the train as well, weren't you? Remember how we woke up and the night just went on and on?

**Platelayer** I do.

**Pokorny** Well, then. Let's hope they don't catch him before he gets up the courage . . .

**Platelayer** (*interrupting him*) Quiet!

*He listens.*

**Pokorny** (*listening as well*) I can hear him . . .

**Platelayer** Here he comes.

*Silence.*

**Pokorny** He's thinking the viaduct's very high, but it might not finish the job . . .

**Platelayer** He's thinking, maybe I should throw myself in front of the train . . .

**Pokorny** Better safe than sorry.

*Hudetz comes slowly in from the left.*
*The Platelayer directs the beam of his lamp at Hudetz. Hudetz stops, very startled.*

**Platelayer** Good evening, Herr Hudetz.

*Hudetz stares at him, terrified.*

I'm just checking the track's all right . . .

*Hudetz sees Pokorny and starts to hurry away.*

**Pokorny** Wait!

*Hudetz stops.*

**Platelayer** Herr Pokorny just wants a word with you . . .

**Pokorny** (*a slight bow*) I'm Pokorny, the engine driver.

**Platelayer** Don't go, we're not going to give you away.

**Hudetz** (*frightened*) Who is that?

73

**Pokorny** I'm the driver of the express train 405, which once had a collision here. Why are you gawping at me like that? You think you can't have a conversation with a dead man? Well, you can, but only if the dead man feels like it . . .

*A short laugh.*

**Platelayer** (*smiling*) Gives you a funny feeling, doesn't it?

**Hudetz** (*suddenly shouting at the Platelayer*) Turn your lamp away, so I can see your face!

**Platelayer** (*calmly*) I don't have a face.

*The wind howls; it sounds like distant trumpets.*
*Hudetz listens carefully.*

**Pokorny** (*to the Platelayer, cheerfully but not without cunning*) Look how frightened he is – and he's got good reason to be, given it's his fault I'm no more.

**Hudetz** (*cutting him off*) It's not.

*Silence.*

**Pokorny** (*approaching Hudetz*) So, you want to escape earthly justice – and you're right! What's the best you could expect? A life sentence?

*Silence.*

**Hudetz** What you're saying is what I've been thinking – but I've thought beyond that.

**Pokorny** (*puzzled*) Beyond it?

**Hudetz** Yes. Because I really am innocent – and if I am going to be judged, I want it to be by a Higher Power. If there is one, if God exists, He'll understand me . . .

**Pokorny** (*grinning*) You said it.

*And now the wind howls, as it did before.*

74

*Hudetz listens carefully, unsettled.*
*Anna comes slowly in from the right and stops.*
*Hudetz looks at her, horrified.*

**Hudetz** Anna!

*Silence.*

**Anna** (*looking straight at Hudetz*) The stationmaster missed a signal . . .

**Pokorny** (*interrupting her*) That was your fault, Fräulein, entirely your fault.

**Platelayer** Is that true?

**Anna** (*as if she were reciting a school exercise*) He forgot the signal because I kissed him, but I would never have kissed him if he hadn't had a wife he never loved . . .

**Pokorny** (*interrupting again*) What's that got to do with it?

**Anna** (*looking straight at Hudetz*) I can't lie any more.

**Hudetz** (*suddenly shouting at her*) Did I invent lying?

*Silence.*

**Anna** (*continuing to stare at Hudetz*) Do you remember when I said to you at the viaduct, 'Now do you recognise me?'

**Hudetz** (*softly*) Yes.

**Anna** And you did recognise me.

**Hudetz** (*uncertainly*) I don't know.

**Anna** I do. You took me in your arms as you had before.

**Hudetz** When?

**Anna** Before, when we were cast out. Heaven came down, in the shape of a severe angel, we heard the words and were afraid to understand them – oh, very afraid –

they were days of sorrow, do you remember? In the sweat of our face . . .

**Hudetz** (*interrupting her*) The guilt was yours! Who was it said to me, 'Take, eat!'?

**Anna** Me.

**Hudetz** And what did I do?

**Anna** (*smiling*) How often have you killed me already and how many more times will you kill me – it doesn't even hurt any more.

**Hudetz** Does that mean you like it?

*Anna shudders and looks at him, horrified.*
*Now the signal bell rings again and the signal changes to green.*

**Platelayer** Train's on its way.

**Pokorny** Late as usual.

**Platelayer** That's right, because it has to wait for the connection . . .

*Hudetz suddenly turns to Pokorny.*

**Hudetz** (*quietly*) Tell me, what's it like over on your side?

**Pokorny** Where we are? Peaceful, very peaceful! You know, like in some quiet country inn, just before it gets dark – there's snow outside and all you can hear is the clock – for ever and ever – you read your paper and drink your beer and never have to pay . . .

**Hudetz** (*smiling*) Really?

**Pokorny** We play cards a lot and everybody wins – or loses, whichever you prefer. We're pretty happy not to be alive any more.

*Express train 405 approaches.*

*They all listen carefully.*

**Pokorny** (*quietly to Hudetz, so that Anna doesn't hear*) Here comes your train . . .

*Hudetz slowly turns towards the embankment.
Anna, frightened, suddenly screams at him.*

**Anna** No!

**Pokorny** (*to Anna*) Don't interfere.

**Hudetz** (*to Anna*) I have an appointment with my colleague, Pokorny.

**Pokorny** We're playing cards.

**Anna** Cards?

**Hudetz** Yes. It's snowing outside, but inside, there's a fire burning and it's warm . . .

**Anna** (*interrupting him*) There's no fire, it isn't warm. Don't believe your colleague. The only reason he came to fetch you is that he's not alive any more and he wants revenge.

**Pokorny** (*to Anna*) Quiet!

**Anna** (*to Hudetz*) I won't be quiet. Oh, please believe me, it's terrible where we are! Stay alive, please stay alive!

**Pokorny** Don't listen to her! The train's coming!

**Anna** (*suddenly clinging on to Hudetz*) Stay alive, please! Stay alive! (*She screams.*) Inspector!

*And now express train 405 thunders by, its whistle blowing. It gets very dark. As the light returns, Hudetz is standing close to the embankment and downstage left are the Policeman, the Landlord, Ferdinand and Alfons. Everyone else has disappeared.*

**Alfons** Thomas!

*Hudetz goes slowly over to the Policeman.*

**Hudetz** I'm giving myself up, Inspector.

**Policeman** You're under arrest.

**Hudetz** (*to Alfons*) I've thought it over . . .

*He nods to him, smiling.*

**Landlord** (*his hand on his heart*) They'll have your head for this, your head . . .

**Hudetz** Maybe. The main thing is not to judge yourself guilty or innocent . . .

*He smiles.*

**Ferdinand** (*suddenly shouting*) Handcuff him, handcuff him!

**Hudetz** No need.

**Ferdinand** Still answering back? Wait till I get at you . . .

*He lunges at him.*

**Alfons** Stop that! Do me a favour and leave him in peace.

**Hudetz** (*to Alfons*) Thanks.

**Policeman** (*to Hudetz*) Come on, then . . .

*The wind howls as before.*
   *Suddenly Hudetz is listening carefully.*

**Hudetz** Listen! (*He listens.*) Can you hear trumpets?

**Alfons** It's only the wind.

*Hudetz nods, smiling, at Alfons.*

**Hudetz** You don't really believe that, do you . . . ?